EIGHTEENTH CENTURY FURNITURE

EIGHTEENTH CENTURY FURNITURE

Grange BOOKS

A QUANTUM BOOK

Published by Grange Books
an imprint of Grange Books Plc
The Grange
Kingsnorth Industrial Estate
Hoo, nr. Rochester
Kent ME3 9ND

1-84013-262-0

This book is produced by
Quantum Books Ltd
6 Blundell Street
London N7 9BH

Project Manager: Rebecca Kingsley
Project Editor: Judith Millidge
Designer: Wayne Humphries
Editor: Clare Haworth-Maden

The material in this publication previously appeared in
Encyclopedia of Furniture

QUM18FT
Set in Times
Reproduced in Singapore by Eray Scan (Pte) Ltd
Printed in Singapore by Star Standard Industries (Pte) Ltd

CONTENTS

INTRODUCTION

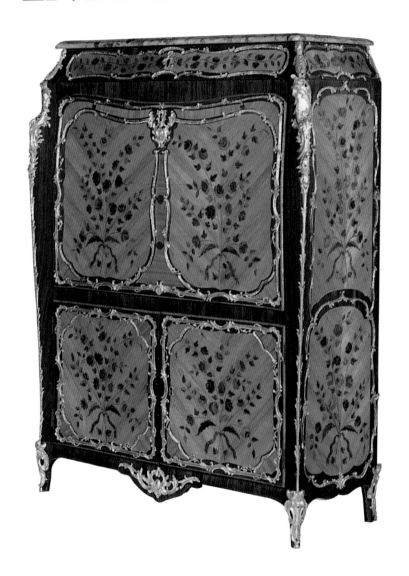

Before 1500 few Europeans had even seen a chair, let alone sat on one; homes – even the great households – were scantily furnished, and what furniture there was simply and sturdily made. It was only during the fifteenth and sixteenth centuries that unified schemes of interior decoration, revealing harmony between architecture, ornamental features, furniture and upholstery began to appear. Furniture was transformed into more heavily worked, highly decorated pieces. The seventeenth century was a time of change, of which perhaps the most significant was that furniture was no longer simply a symbol of power and status – it had become the property of the populace. While the seventeenth century had been marked by its variety of furniture forms, especially tables, the eighteenth century is noted for its craftsmanship, and new craftsmen and designers in America emerged as a force to be reckoned with.

Opposite: A French Louis XV secrétaire à abattant. The secrétaire à abattant first came into fashion as a large piece of case furniture in the 1750s, and examples like this are quite rare. This tulipwood-veneered example shows all the features of later more typical secrétaires of the Louis XVI period.

Below: An English 'French Hepplewhite' bergère c. 1770. This chair is typical of the style imported from France. Designed to support an ample frame the chairs have become part of the back and it is clearly different from the open armchairs and wing chairs which preceded it.

FRENCH RÉGENCE AND LOUIS XV STYLES

Furniture of the Régence and Louis XV (1715-74) periods rejected the weighty and grandiose, becoming more graceful and with exuberant but simplified Rococo curves. This tendency appeared in the last years of Louis XIV's reign and was reinforced during the first eight years of Louis XV's reign (a period known as the Régence).

Plain wood veneer replaced boulle marquetry and gilt-bronze ornamentation was simplified. Curvilinear motifs, such as water, plants, dragons and shells, proliferated in carved wood, marquetry and gilt bronze, and the structure of pieces became all but invisible. Seat and architectural furniture, such as console tables and mirrors, was made of beech or walnut, invisibly joined or pegged and gilded, or else painted to harmonise with the rest of the room. The carcasses of case furniture were often made cheaply from pine, or sometimes oak, and were veneered with exotic woods in geometric patterns known as parquetry.

DECORATIVE FEATURES

By the 1740s, flower marquetry had become popular. Veneering was sometimes carried out with lacquer, Japanese or Chinese, or a French imitation known as "vernis Martin". Case furniture also incorporated gilt-bronze mounts as ornaments on projecting corners and on feet, as handles and as frames for marquetry panels.

NEW FURNITURE STYLES

Many new types and shapes of furniture appeared during Louis XV's reign. The most common style of chair, the fauteuil (armchair), had a scrolled, heart-shaped seat and back, and curved legs and armrests. If the back was flat, it was a fauteuil à la reine; if it was curved, it was a fauteuil en cabriolet. The bergère (easy chair) was large and comfortable and had upholstery under, as well as on

top of, the armrests. Console tables stood on exaggeratedly curved legs, which would be decorated perhaps with foliage on the legs themselves and a basket of flowers or Rococo scroll on the stretchers.

The commode was the principal piece of case furniture of the period. It had a curved front, sides and legs and either two or three rows of drawers. The bureau plat competed with various new types of desk, such as the secrétaire à abattant (fall-front writing desk), which had two doors and a writing-surface flap that pulled down to reveal small drawers inside.

THE TRANSITIONAL STYLE

Towards the end of Louis XV's reign, Rococo style gradually gave way to neo-classical ornamentation, a style known as Transitional. It was characterised by the use of classical architectural forms and motifs, such as straight lines, symmetry, pilaster, fluting, rosettes, lion

Right: A French Louis XVI gilt wood canapé by Georges Jacob c.1775. This canapé is part of a set, but the sofa's frame is in complete contrast to the rounded chair backs. The frame is carved with leaf tips in a continuous laurel banding. It stands on circular fluted legs that taper and are headed by paterae and gadrooned capitals.

masks and leaf or bead mouldings. At first furniture was curvilinear in the familiar Rococo style, but it acquired neo-classical ornamentation. Then the shapes began to incorporate neo-classical elements – commodes became rectilinear, for example – while the heart-shaped backs of seat furniture were often supported on straight legs. The neo-classical shapes came to be increasingly decorated in the same style. The body of the commode, for example, was adorned with formal flower marquetry and a scroll frieze.

By about 1770 neo-classicism had almost completely superseded the Rococo. Classical forms and motifs were not, however, applied to interior decoration with great seriousness. They were used in a fanciful way that produced an elegant style that was well suited to the light architectural interiors of the day.

THE LOUIS XVI STYLE

In the reign of Louis XVI (1774-93) furniture was mainly adapted from earlier pieces and few new types were introduced. (Among the few new pieces to emerge at this time was the console d'ébéniste, which was supported on column legs.) Seat furniture lost all traces of the Rococo and case furniture acquired an angular look. Pictorial marquetry continued to be used on case furniture, but gradually plain veneer, especially in mahogany, began to supplant marquetry. Plaques of Sèvres porcelain were also applied to case furniture

THE DIRECTOIRE AND EMPIRE STYLES

The years following the French Revolution of 1789 were turbulent. The political upheavals were mirrored by artistic ones. The dissolution of the guilds had a dramatic effect on furniture-making. In addition, the difficult economic conditions of the times imposed austerity on a hitherto luxurious craft. Elaborate veneered and gilt-bronze-mounted pieces were no longer commercially possible, and as a result

simple, painted furniture was made.

The style of design prevalent from *c.*1793 to 1804 is known as Directoire, after the French Directorate. Its principal characteristic was the use of arabesque and Etruscan forms and motifs, such as fanciful animals, eagles, serpents, lozenges and palmettes.

The personal influence on the arts of the emperor, Napoleon Bonaparte, was considerable. He encouraged the development of a monumental style, based on massive, solid shapes and bold decoration. The main source of inspiration for the Empire style was the heavy, carved marble outdoor furniture of the Graeco-Roman world. Another major influence was Egypt. Artists had travelled in Napoleon's expedition to that country in 1799 and recorded what they saw, beginning a craze in France for anything Egyptian.

BRITISH FURNITURE

One of the hallmarks that characterise the furniture of the early eighteenth century was a lack of pretension. Simple oak chairs, stools, chests and tables were made well into the eighteenth century. The details of a chair back or the panels of a chest might differ from seventeenth century examples, but the basic type altered little. Although often attractive and always useful, these pieces were not stylistically important – it was the furniture made for royal palaces and great houses that set new trends.

EVOLUTION AND INNOVATION

One of the most important pieces to evolve

Left: A French bureau à cylindre of the Louis XVI period. Elegant cylinder desks of this type superseded the more basic slope-front desks in fashionable circles in the second half of the century.

Above: Queen Anne oval stool c.1710. Plain elegant curves with immeasurable harmony of line show the hand of a master at work.

in the early eighteenth century, by way of the chest on a stand and the chest-on-chest (tallboy), was the large bureau cabinet. Such pieces were designed to grace the salons of gracious houses, and were given the most lavish treatment, including veneers of strongly figured or burr woods, together with japanning in brilliant red or lustrous black, with gold, Chinese-style ornamentation (chinoiserie) in relief.

An innovation of the Queen Anne and early Georgian periods was a proliferation of small, well-made pieces, such as tables for taking tea or displaying china or needlework. Dressing tables, small chests of drawers – known as bachelor's chests – small kneehole desks and small cupboards and cabinets for displaying china were also popular.

What has come to be known as Queen Anne (reigned 1702-14) style is most closely associated with the evolution of the cabriole (double curved) leg. The H-shaped stretchers of the earliest cabriole-legged chairs were soon abandoned, and both tables and chairs stood on gently serpentine legs terminating in pad feet. More robust curves developed later, and knees or bulges at the tops of legs were often decorated with carved shell medallions. By George I's reign (1714-27), feet were usually of the lion's paw or ball-and-claw variety.

PALLADIAN TO ROCOCO

The Palladian movement of the 1720s and 1730s, which reflected a revival of classic Roman styles, coincided with a gradual transition from walnut to mahogany. The luster and strength of mahogany made it the ideal material to be used for chairs, which were ornamented with crisply carved motifs, and for the architecturally conceived furniture of William Kent and his contemporaries.

Even as the sober discipline of classical form was being promoted by the supporters of Palladian principles, the French Rococo was gaining ground in England, a move encouraged by both the influx of immigrant craftsmen and the increasing availability of pattern books depicting the work of leading French designers. The new ideas took root in cabinet-making, and furniture began to show the restless, asymmetrical twists and curves of the Rococo.

THOMAS CHIPPENDALE

Thomas Chippendale (1718-79) devoted his life to producing beautiful and robust furniture, and his pattern book *The Gentleman and Cabinet-Maker's Director* (1754, 1755, and 1759-62) revolutionised furniture-making in

Below: An English George I walnut settle c.1725. The flat uprights with a little carved decoration and low seat make this piece easy to date. The cabriole legs have typically shell-carved knees and ball-and-claw feet, popular at the time.

Britain. It was the first design book to cover all kinds of furniture, and its success in distilling the current styles of decoration into a form that was both workable for the cabinet-maker and acceptable to his clients led to the adoption of the name 'Chippendale' as a generic label for mid-eighteenth century furniture. Practically all the furniture covered in the pattern book alludes to the Rococo.

NEO-CLASSICISM

Fashions changed quickly in eighteenth century England. The Rococo flowered late and briefly. No sooner had the smartest houses been fitted out with 'French' chairs, lacquered or marquetry bombé commodes and fantas-tically carved and gilded mirrors, than the new classicism was being urged.

Classical ideals were already well rooted in England, most recently through the Palladian movement, whose archaeologically-based designs remained fundamental to much furni-ture in the 1750s. Archaeological discoveries at Herculaneum and Pompeii during the mid-eighteenth century coincided with a decline of interest in Rococo ornament and generated a new fascination with classical antiquity. For the remainder of the eighteenth century and for the first decade of the nineteenth century there was a striving towards greater archae-ological accuracy in classical interpretation.

ROBERT ADAM

No designer was more important in dissemi-nating the neo-classical style than Robert Adam (1728-92). He had acquired his knowledge of classical design during the years he spent in Italy, and his subsequent employment by many of the richest and most powerful property owners in Britain gave him immense prestige and wide influence. In his all-embracing

approach to building schemes, in partnership with his brothers John (1721-92) and James (1732-94), he took responsibility for all aspects of interior decoration, including the furniture. Among the cabinet-makers who collaborated with him were Thomas Chippendale, John Linnell (1729-96), William Ince (d. 1804) and John Mayhew (*fl.* 1758-1804), William Vile (*c.* 1700-67), John Cobb (*c.*1715-78) and Samuel Norman (*fl.* 1746-67).

The light elegance of the Adam style was

Below: An English George III satinwood Hepplewhite dressing table c.1780. Of typical neo-classical design, this piece also incorporates elements of French style in the cabriole legs and on the edges of the table.

Below: George II gilt armchairs in the style of Robert Adam, 1780. With their oval backs and nicely carved legs, these chairs are archetypal Adam.

well suited to the domestic interior and enhanced the skills of the furniture craftsman, giving unprecedented scope for marquetry decoration. The asymmetrical flourishes of Rococo plaster-work were translated on furniture into well-regulated borders of anthemion or paterae, scrolled acanthus, looped garlands and graceful arabesques. Painting and gilding were also widely used, and decorative ceramic plaques as well as finely chiselled gilt-bronze mounts were applied to surfaces veneered in finely figured mahogany or satinwood.

The style was distilled most successfully in *The Cabinet-Maker and Upholsterer's Guide* (1788), the posthumously published design book by George Hepplewhite (d. 1786), which took the Adam style not only to the furthest corners of Britain but to many parts of North America and Europe. Hepplewhite's express aim 'to unite elegance and utility' was fulfilled in nearly 300 patterns.

THOMAS SHERATON

The late eighteenth and early nineteenth centuries was a time known in English furniture as the Sheraton period, after the designer Thomas Sheraton (1751-1806).

Relatively little is known of Sheraton's working life. Unlike Chippendale and Hepplewhite, he probably never had a workshop of his own, although he must have been trained as a cabinet-maker. His first pattern book, *The Cabinet-Maker and Upholsterer's Drawing Book* (1791-94) echoes the distinctly francophile neo-classicism of the architect Henry Holland (1745-1806). The pattern book was seen as a digest of the most refined neo-classical taste and, like Hepplewhite's, influenced furniture all over Europe, as well as in America and Britain.

THE NETHERLANDS AND ANGLO-DUTCH STYLE

In the late seventeenth and early eighteenth centuries, when Dutch influence on English furniture was particularly strong, the Dutch in turn absorbed what they liked about English styles and types. The result was what has come to be known as Anglo-Dutch style: caning for

chairs, for example, was a Dutch introduction that became popular in England. Dutch cabinet-makers became leaders in the new craft of veneering and developed a specialised form of this – floral marquetry. One of the first and greatest exponents of the art was Jan van Mekeren (*fl. c.*1690-*c.*1735) of Amsterdam, much of whose work was exported. The Dutch passion for porcelain led to the invention of the glass-fronted display cabinet. Corner cupboards, some with lacquered panels in the doors, were also used for displaying china. Both types were adopted in England.

Daniel Marot (1663-1752), spent his formative years studying the Baroque style of the French court in Paris, and then successfully transposed it to The Netherlands. His furniture was sculptural in inspiration and he was an important contributor to the Anglo-Dutch style. But by the 1720s his heavy style was being supplanted by the lighter exuberance of the Rococo. With the onset of neo-classicism, the extravagantly veneered decoration that had been such a feature of Dutch furniture became more restrained.

The fashion for both French and English furniture continued in the second half of the eighteenth-century, to the extent that Dutch cabinet-makers felt that their livelihoods were being threatened by imports. In 1771 the protests of the Amsterdam Guild resulted in a ban on all foreign imports of furniture. During

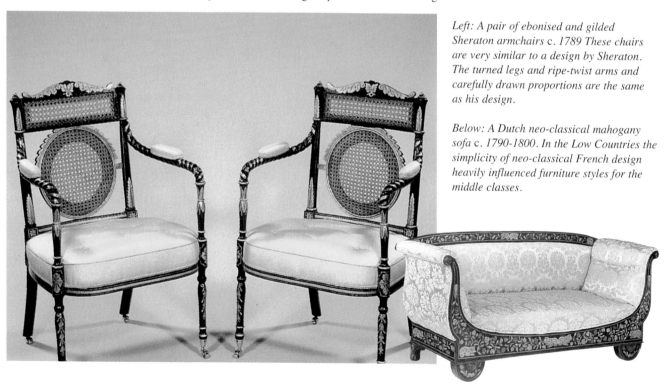

Left: A pair of ebonised and gilded Sheraton armchairs c. *1789 These chairs are very similar to a design by Sheraton. The turned legs and ripe-twist arms and carefully drawn proportions are the same as his design.*

Below: A Dutch neo-classical mahogany sofa c. *1790-1800. In the Low Countries the simplicity of neo-classical French design heavily influenced furniture styles for the middle classes.*

the last decades of the eighteenth century, when Dutch cabinet-makers were especially prosperous, a French-inspired version of neo-classicism prevailed.

ITALIAN FURNITURE

While the emphasis in northern Europe tended to be on solid quality and good craftsman-ship, many Italian pieces from this period are colorfully embellished but shoddily constructed. The enthusiasm for oriental lacquer was shared by the Italians, but Italian furniture-makers not only adopted japanning as an alternative, but also developed their own method of imitating its effect. The technique known as lacca povera (or lacca contrafatta) involved pasting cut-out and painted pictures on the painted surfaces of furniture and then lavishly coating the whole with varnish. Painting was another favourite form of furni-ture decoration.

SPANISH AND PORTUGUESE FURNITURE

The furniture of eighteenth-century Spain and Portugal was rich in references to colonial expansion and cultural cross-currents. In Spain the influence of France and Italy continued to dominate, but Moorish traditions lived on in provincial and country furniture. In the first half of the eighteenth century, furni-ture imported from England influenced Spanish design, particularly of chairs. Japanned pieces were popular imports and early Georgian and Chippendale designs were translated by the Spanish into walnut or poplar, or given carved and gilded Rococo orna-

Left: A walnut German bureau-cabinet, c.1740 Although the marquetry of this piece is still baroque, the bombé shape and rocaille scrolls give a hint of Rococo.

mentation and H-form stretchers. Later, Hepplewhite and Sheraton designs were echoed, but less obviously.

In Portugal, English influence was most powerful. When the widowed consort of King Charles II, Catherine of Braganza, returned to her native Portugal in 1693, she took English furniture with her. The fashion she introduced was reinforced by mercantile treaties that resulted in large consignments of English furniture finding their way into Portuguese homes. In many examples, English taste merged with French Rococo influence, but the interpretations were distinctly Portuguese and were often carried out in non-European woods, such as the hard, dark jacaranda that was imported from Brazil.

GERMAN FURNITURE

Germany's long tradition of wood carving continued in much of the furniture produced during the eighteenth century, but from the early eighteenth century veneers were increasingly used. The seeds of the Rococo were being sown by certain princes in Germany, even though the Baroque showed little sign of fading from favour for the majority.

RUSSIAN FURNITURE

In Russia the most fashionable European furniture styles were enthusiastically adopted for palaces and country houses. In the late seventeenth century Russia began importing fine-quality pieces and having them copied by craftsmen in local woods. A mix of mid-European styles and Russian characteristics developed during the eighteenth century.

It was the French Rococo that had the greatest direct impact on the furnishing of Russian palaces. It was largely introduced between 1716 and 1726 by the French sculptor

and woodcarver Nicolas Pineau (1684-1754), one of the leading exponents of Rococo design, who was commissioned by Peter the Great (reigned 1682-1725). Neo-classicism was introduced by the Scottish architect Charles Cameron (c.1743-1812), who worked for Catherine the Great (reigned 1762-96) from the late 1770s, furniture being supplied by the most fashionable Parisian ébénistes.

FURNITURE IN SCANDINAVIA

Painted furniture – of birch, beech or ash, as well as pine – was characteristic of Scandinavian houses. Even so, Sweden and Norway were as open as any other country to stylistic developments in Europe. The English demand for timber to reconstruct London after the Great Fire of 1666 brought both prosperity and English furniture design to Scandinavia in the late seventeenth century, and because English design was itself affected by the Dutch, Scandinavian furniture of the period is distinctly Anglo-Dutch.

Because of its geographical proximity, Germany also strongly affected Scandinavian furniture types and styles and the Rococo in Scandinavia tended to be interpreted in its Germanic form, especially in Denmark and Norway. Sweden was more francophile, and Paris-trained architects dominated the introduction of the style into the salons of Stockholm in the 1730s and 1740s.

French influence on Denmark became strong in the neo-classical period, largely through the appointment of the French sculptor Jacques-François Saly (1717-96) as director of the new Copenhagen Academy. In Sweden, where neo-classicism was adopted later than in Denmark, its interpretation included both French and English elements.

Above: An English George III mahogany artist's table c. 1790. This baize-lined table has a lighter frame than most. The double ratchet mechanism withdraws into a custom-made cover, secured by a loop. When folded, the table covers an aperture to hold a palette, and the under tier is shaped to fit the knees of the artist.

THE AMERICAN STYLE

The term 'colonial furniture' is used broadly to refer to pieces made before 1775. Before the War of Independence, design influences came from England and Europe generally. Each nationality of immigrant, especially the Dutch, brought not only pieces of furniture but also affection for a traditional national style. These influences combined to create a recognizably 'American' style.

AMERICAN QUEEN ANNE STYLE

In the United States the term 'Queen Anne' is generally used to describe pieces made between *c.* 1715 and 1750. The graceful lines and elegant carving of this style were a revelation to the Americans, who found that the appearance of the pieces fitted well with the new colonial sense of expansion and prosperity. Perhaps the artistic high point of the style was the highboy, a chest of drawers with the upper,

taller section standing on a lower section with legs; the highboy was soon joined by the lowboy – the lower section of the taller piece.

CHIPPENDALE STYLE

Some elements of Chippendale's work had appeared in American pieces during the 1730s and 1740s, but it was not until the 1760s that the full force of his work struck the fashion-conscious inhabitants of American cities. The finest Santo Domingo mahogany was used to embody his ideas, and walnut never recovered in popularity.

Philadelphia was the capital of furniture-making in the Chippendale style, and New York, Boston and Salem followed its lead. The cabinet-makers that worked there produced chairs, highboys and bureau-bookcases that were more crisply executed than their English equivalents, with less extravagant curves. The flame finials, frequently seen on the pediments of secretaries and highboys, and the peanut carving enlivening the top rails and aprons of chairs, mark these pieces out as uniquely American.

It was the craftsmen of Rhode Island and Connecticut who offered more serious alternatives to Philadelphia's dominance. The vigorous forms of the Queen Anne style, still alive there, were effortlessly integrated into the new style. Deceptively simple, yet majestic, block-front desks, secretaries and chest of drawers made by these areas' leading craftsmen have become as distinctly American in character as the highboy.

Above: An American Federal period mahogany veneered secretary bookcase. Although this scroll-topped writing desk owes a debt to the Chippendale style, it also anticipates several features of the later Federal period. It was made in Salem in the last 20 years of the century.

Left: An American Chippendale wing chair c.1780 This is very much a transitional chair: parts resemble Queen Anne style, but the legs and stretchers are typical Chippendale.

SEATING

From the earliest of times, chairs and sofas were divided into the purely functional seats or settles, and the more elegant and imposing throne for those in power - namely royalty, church and the law. Refinement of design was clearly a force where there was money to be spent, and patronage of the arts and of craftsman produced beautiful as well as functional items. Just as trade increased contact between different cultures, so political turbulence was responsible for the exchange of ideas within it. The eighteenth century saw a tremendous cross-fertilization of ideas with, for the first time, pattern books from great cabinet-makers detailing design proposals. Armchairs had their arms set back to accompany the hooped dresses of the period, and lounging became so popular,that the sofa and chaise-longue developed too.

Previous page: A George II giltwood armchair, c. 1750. This is one of a set of eight armchairs and a sofa, and displays all the best aspects of English rococo. With a design heavily indebted to Louis XV's court, it is a small, light chair. The arms are swept upwards on leafy scrolls, and this pattern is echoed on the four cabriole legs which end in scrolls at the toe. The rich effect created by the gilt underframe is countered by the severe shape of the upholstery, which gives an overall balance to the chair.

INFLUENCES

Although France was obviously the dominant influence over taste at the beginning of the eighteenth century, different political climates did introduce their own styles. Rococo was the style of the time, with veneers, marquetry, ormolu mounts and oriental lacquer. In France two main styles of chair prevailed: the siège meuble, immovable and set against a wall, and the lighter siège courant, which could be moved as and when required.

In England the early eighteenth century was a period of sobriety, the basis of the Queen Anne style, with its higher backed chairs and with vertical lines and plain splats. As well as the evolution of the cabriole leg, the backs of Queen Anne and early Georgian chairs were serpentine in outline, with vase-shaped splats of well-figured walnut or carved shells at the top. Upholstered

seats added colour, while japanned chairs, which were more or less the same overall shape, usually had caned seats and backs.

The Georgian period (1714-1779) found its main medium in the mahogany imported from the West Indies, which overtook walnut in popularity by 1750. The use of mahogany encouraged the return to carved decoration and this can be seen in the work of Thomas Chippendale.

From the 1720s chair backs became less elongated, so that by the 1750s they were a squat, rectangular shape, slightly flaring at the top. The top rails, which often terminated in projecting 'ears', and the pierced back splat were carved into sinuous organic forms, or geometric Chinese patterns. All the designs were echoed in the carving on the knees and front cabriole legs. Scrolled feet were more fashionable than ball-and-claw or pad feet at this time. Some chairs from this period have straight front legs decorated with fluting or carved borders and reinforcing stretchers. Seats were generally upholstered, but narrow-backed 'hall' chairs usually had wooden seats.

More comfortable sets of chairs were made for gentlemen's houses. Side chairs had shaped seats and rounded backs, upholstered in brightly coloured needlework, sometimes with arms of sinuous a walnut. Most luxurious of all were the all-over upholstered and cushioned wing chairs.

Opposite page: A mid-eighteenth century chair-back settee in the manner of Thomas Chippendale. This design is a classic of its kind. It is little more than two chairs joined together and is notable for its elegance, rather than comfort. The chairs are typical Chippendale with elaborate interlaced ribbon backs, leafy rails all on gothic triple-column front legs. The importance of this design is that it is a stepping-stone between the love seat and the fully upholstered sofa we have today.

Left: A pair of Queen Anne japanned chairs c. 1710. The style of these chairs draws from fashions immediately before and after this date. The chair's curves are very gentle, with the elegant cabriole legs giving outwards as much below the knee as above thus creating a restful balance which ends on a square foot.

Below: A George II giltwood armchair c.1750 by the cabinet maker William Gordon. This chair is part of a considerable suite and is typical of the style of the mid-eighteenth century. William Gordon primarily worked with another craftsman John Tait. The suit is representative of the Rococo style which remained more restrained than the European styles. Here the rails are curved, the legs cabriole on scrolling feet and almost every surface is carved.

Above: A pair of George II Gainsborough armchairs c. 1756 These fine mid-century examples of comfortable armchairs by John Gordon were of a style supplied to a number of great houses at the time. Although they are of the same comfortable proportions as armchairs of today, they are of an unusual design. The arm supports down to the seat seem to emulate a dolphin motif found on contemporary French and Italian chairs, here delightfully understated. The seat rail cupid's bow alludes to the classical motifs of an earlier period and sweeps down into the simple cabriole legs with the nicely detailed leaf. The fish-scale decoration is also from the organic baroque vocabulary of the late seventeenth century.

Chairs with upholstered backs and seats were known as French chairs, whether they were round-contoured, cabriole legged variety with frames carved and gilded in the French Rococo manner, or of the minimally ornamented, squarish-backed type that are now often called Gainsborough chairs.

The second half of the century saw a move towards European design influences, especially neo-classicism. By the end of the century English chair designs were imported copied, adapted and widely admired in countries throughout the world, from America to Russia, Norway to Spain.

REGIONAL FURNITURE

During the early eighteenth century, there came into widespread use a type of chair known as the Windsor Chair. Characterised by a solid wooden seat, simple turned legs, and a stick back, this robust form of seating gave rise to a host of regional variations. These Windsor, or stick-back chairs were only part of a rich rural tradition of chair making that includes spindle- and ladder-back chairs of the Midlands and northern England, and the button-back chairs of East Anglia. These styles of chairs were governed more by geography than by period fashions.

Because the new styles eventually percolated downwards through the social strata, regional or traditional chairs often displayed the characteristic decorative features of 'town' furniture, such as padded feet, cabriole legs, and vase-shaped splats. Some East Anglian chairs can be associated with known Sheraton designs. Even so, most regional chairs were built for durability rather than elegance, and their legs are usually reinforced by stretchers. Furniture for the middle and lower classes was expected to last rather longer than the latest

Below: A Régence walnut armchair c.1715 This fauteuil has many seventeenth century continental characteristics: the curving x-framed stretchers, cabriole legs, hoofed feet and gently curving arms. Scallops on the arms are echoed by the scallops and trellis work on the arm rails. The mellow combination of the warm colored walnut against the tapestry upholstery represents an elegant high point in neo-baroque European furniture.

Above: English chair c.1850. This is a good, if slightly late example of the Windsor chair and represents the final stages of the development of the style. The back is of yew and the seat of elm. By this time the style incorporated the Victorian habit of turning.

Below: A giltwood bergère 1764 An impressive bergère – a French term for an upholstered armchair with upholstered sides. While still showing some Rococo curves, the basic chair shape has been straightened to become more expansive and cubic, a little more neo-classical. It is on this type of chair that Robert Adam and other English designers based their own versions.

fashionable fads popular with the upper classes.

FRENCH DESIGNS

The period known as the Régence (1715-23) corresponds to the first few years of George I's reign in England. In England the designs had changed rather sharply from the highly decorated period of William and Mary to the restrained and simple designs developed in the reign of Queen Anne. However, in France the late seventeenth century styles matured smoothly in the early eighteenth century, to open, elegant neo-baroque European furniture.

Louis XV's succession to the French throne in 1723 introduced the lighter more elegant Rococo style. With Louis XVI and Marie Antoinette on the throne in 1774, the flat surfaces and linear shapes decorated with lacquer and ormolu drew heavily on classical influences The 1780s saw a vogue for English design and neo-classicism and Rococo merged until the traumatic Revolution of 1789. From then until the end of the century plainer Directoire furniture was seen. Seat furniture was usually painted in light colours at this time. Legs were often shaped like sabres or cornucopias or were turned and tapering (but not usually fluted). Backs were open-work with the top rail curling like a scroll.

The influence of Napoleon was considerable. He encouraged the development of a monumental style based on solid shapes and bold decoration. The Empire style was inspired by the carved marble furniture of the Graeco-Roman world. Seat furniture was made either of mahogany or gilt wood. With their square backs and boldly-carved front legs arising from the armrests, such seats appear to have been designed to fit in an imposing interior rather than with the comfort of the sitter in mind.

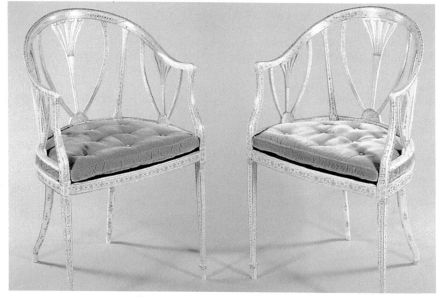

Below: An American Queen Anne walnut chair c. 1840. A typical example, the scrolls on this chair have an extraordinary sinuous effect, and the splat is finely figured to create a delightful combination of simplicity and decoration.

OTHER EUROPEAN DESIGN INFLUENCES

In other parts of Europe the English influence was notable. In Portugal chairs most often reflected the English style, but were more exuberantly carved and usually had H-shaped stretchers. In many examples, English tastes merged with French, and were then carried out in non-European woods such as hard, dark jacaranda which was imported from Brazil.

In northern Germany, English and Dutch characteristics were visible in cabriole legs, shaped backs and caned seats and back panels. The style was popular into the mid-eighteenth century. Dutch and English chairs ran a parallel course in development. The burgomaster or roundabout chair was imported from the East Indies into the Netherlands during the late seventeenth century and early eighteenth century. It had a round caned seat, low back with carved splat, and turned supports; the

Above: A pair of Anglo-Indian George III ivory chairs c.1790. During the late seventeenth century Anglo-Indian furniture consisted mostly of cabinets and caskets of local woods inlaid with figurative and geometric designs. By the end of the eighteenth century a move towards elegant designs and a taste for dramatically-coloured furniture brought forth a variety of ivory veneered objects. India under British rule produced some veneered furniture based on contemporary British designs. These particular chairs are made from solid ivory. Of considerable weight, the Hepplewhite-style frame is painted with orientalised gilt foliage.

carved cabriole legs were united by turned stretchers. Dutch examples, usually of walnut or oak, and Indian versions were exported and copied usually in lighter form by English chair makers.

AMERICAN DEVELOPMENT

The growth of the industry and trade links with America increased the exchange of ideas with Europe. The William and Mary-style chair, popular at the beginning of the century began to merge with more sophisticated Queen Anne chair designs around 1725, and American Queen Anne chair designs showed the style at its best. The graceful lines and appearance fitted in well with the new colonial sense of expansion and prosperity.

Comfort was an established factor in chair design. The upholstered wing chair with tall back, face-level fire protector and rolled arms was introduced. On this the turnkeywork and velvet of the previous century were supplanted by silk, damask and wool. More popular were the wooden settees and day-beds with bowed top rails.

The American Windsor chair first appeared in c.1725. It differed from the English version in the lack of a back splat and exaggerated angle at which the legs were set to the seat. This, combined with the large number of spindles used to form the back, made the American Windsor chair feel lighter. Two styles were common: the bow back in which the top rail was bent into a three-quarter hoop and the

Left: American Windsor chair c.1750 This is a good example of a rustic Carver chair, based on a design supposedly brought to America by John Carver the first governor of the then British colony.

Right: A Philadelphia Chippendale chair c. 1775. Primarily made of mahogany, but including some pine, this chair is an excellent example of Philadelphia carving. Although the motifs are based on nature, they appear as tight parallel curves or outwards moving lines which are very striking.

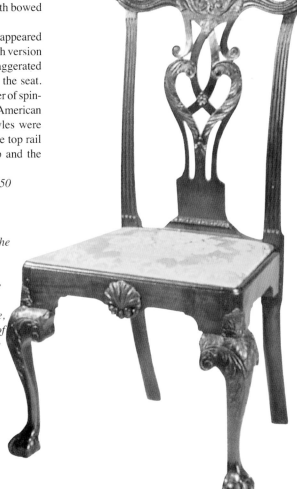

Left: A French Louis XV gilt-wood canapé c. 1725-30. The term 'canapé' refers to high-backed French sofa in the Louis XV style, although it is also used to describe a sofa with closed sides. The serpentine top rail is carved with flower heads and scrolling acanthus leaves, flanked by shells and wave motifs. It is also decorated on the reverse The armrests are carved with foliage, shells and incised with lattice work.

Below: An English Georgian oak settle c. 1750-60. This is typical of the settles made for use in large halls. A simple design, it has unusual turned arms supports. The single squab cushion rest on wooden slats although in some versions cord was strung across the seat. There are many variations on this basic form as country makers in each area made these very practical pieces in some number.

Right: A French George I mahogany love seat with needlework upholstery c. 1720. Small-sized sofas such as this one were known as love seats and were ideal for the display of needlework. The mahogany sofa has a shaped back and high scrolled arms with curvilinear supports.

Below right: A French Régence beech-wood sofa with needlework upholstery c. 1720. Early eighteenth century French Régence furniture was lighter and more sophisticated than its British counterpart. The delicacy of the its scrolled legs joined by waved cross-stretchers carved with flowers is typical of the best work made within the guild system which encouraged the development of the various crafts involved in the construction of seat furniture.

comb back in which the rail was almost straight.

The variety of skills required in chair making (upholstery, carving, turning, joining) reached their height in Philadelphia in the mid-eighteenth century. The influence of Thomas Chippendale arrived in America around 1760, and his name is synonymous with Rococo in American design. New England Chippendale is much more linear than English Chippendale, and different areas show distinct stylistic characteristics. Regional variations are complex and well documented.

The popularity of decorated European styles was greatly accelerated by the arrival of Thomas Affleck from London in 1763. He worked with Philadelphians such as William Savery, James Gillingham, John Shoemaker and the celebrated Benjamin Randolph. American Chippendale indulged in more curves and sculptural form (such as universal ball and claw feet) than the English style, and

Below: A design for an English George II sofa by Thomas Chippendale c. 1759. One of Chippendale's most elegant designs published in 1759, the suggested dimensions are 6ft to 9ft long, 2ft to 3ft in depth and 1ft to 2ft high (including castors). Chippendale recommended that the seats should be deep enough for the sofa to be used as an occasional bed.

seemed more continental in flavour. Pieces tended to be on a large scale, especially those from the Delaware River Valley, which are sometime rather plain. The link with central Europe is particularly evident in Pennsylvanian rustic furniture with its decorative bias.

The American Revolution interrupted the flow of ideas from Europe, but Robert Adam's designs provided the base for the Classical revival seen from about 1780 in the United States.

SOFAS, SETTLES AND DAY-BEDS

Because of their size, all sofas were relatively expensive items, their construction relying upon good quality hardwood that was necessary for strength. The costliest versions were those with detailed carving or inlay. In the early part of the century, the most progressive seat furniture was made for the great houses and palaces, but by the 1760s up-to-date designs for the homes of gentlefolk of moderate means became available. The gradual shift in emphasis from the taste of the nobility to the middle-classes resulted in an increase in the number of manufacturers, many of whom are known through the labels and marks they applied to the sofa frames. French furniture enthusiasts are especially fortunate, since after 1751, every item was required to be stamped with the maker's name, a system that was not enforced in Britain or America.

SUITES

Some of the most splendid eighteenth century sofas were designed as components of large suites of furniture. Intent on creating interiors of perfection, architects such as William Kent developed furniture styles that were in accord with the structure of the room; thus tables, stools and a massive pair of sofas were all

Right: A French Louis XV giltwood day-bed by Jean-Baptiste Tilliard, late eighteenth century. This ornate, typically French day-bed of carved and gilded wood bears the stamp of Jean-Baptiste Tilliard (1688-1766). The apron decoration echoes that of the back. The drop-in squab cushions were probably filled with curled horse-hair and provided the comfort demanded by buyers at the time. Tilliard was among the leading craftsmen of his day.

*Below: American mahogany day bed
c. 1740-50. The eight legs on this day-bed
identify it as a transitional piece, part
William and Mary-style, part Queen Anne.
The bow back with its flanking spindles
harks back to earlier influences and a
multi-arm stretcher connects the legs.*

conceived as part of a grand composition. Kent dominated the fashionable taste of the early years of the century.

By the 1750s sofas were an accepted part of any gentleman's house and there were various styles for the hall, drawing-room, boudoir, or library. The simplest were given drop-in seats and wooden backs, a type that remained in popular use for entrance halls until the twentieth century. The chair back type of sofa, first seen in the seventeenth century was

popular, but some more interesting pieces were upholstered in needlepoint depicting Biblical or classical scenes. Most of this needlework was produced commercially, but occasional sets of gros- and petit-point covers were worked by ladies of the house.

From his pattern book, we know that Chippendale designed some upholstered sofas, which were increasingly comfortable rather than just decorative. For additional comfort he suggested a matching bolster at

each end, as well as square back cushions. However, his more opulent designs which included gilded, carved cherubs and classical figures as the decorative features, were deemed necessary for splendid rooms. Chippendale's couches were in fact comfortable armchairs with the seats extended and supported on six or eight legs, and these are among the most elegant of sofa designs.

EUROPEAN STYLE

In eighteenth century Europe, French furniture styles were all important. Sofas made in the Rue de Cléry area of Paris were exported to Germany and Russia for the homes of the most discerning clients. These sofas, made of oak, beech or walnut, were polished, painted or gilded. Among the large variety of sofa styles created was the curved confidant or tête-à-tête on which two or three people sat

facing in opposite directions enabling them to whisper discreetly. Such pieces often formed part of a large suite of salon furniture which could also include several sofas and lits de repos, all upholstered in Gobelins tapestry of ravishing Lyons silk.

The age of Revolution in Europe heralded simpler antique forms once used by the Egyptians and Greeks. Restrained fabrics were used as being more suited to the new democratic lifestyle. Although seen as the most refined in Europe, Britain and American designers favoured the cleaner, more academic line which revealed the quality of the workmanship rather than obscuring it with ornament.

UPHOLSTERY

The part played by the upholsterer in history has been somewhat neglected. In the

Bottom left: English bed, carved and gilded wood c.1756. This bed, probably made by James Norman, is hung with red damask and represents the late flowering of Rococo style. The domed top, gilded cornice and matching wall hangings, fire guards and bed hangings are typical of the period.

Bottom right: A French Empire bird's-eye maple sofa, 1790s. The severe form of this sofa dated from the Republican period. The light-colored woods, such as maple were also favored by the Germans. The use of flat shapes and curves in a single plane was common to progressive furniture makers in both countries.

eighteenth century the upholsterer was concerned not just with the seat upholstery, but also with bed hangings, wall and floor coverings, window blinds and curtains, and was also usually responsible for the arrangement of furniture in the room.

A heavy emphasis was placed on textiles and during the seventeenth, eighteenth and nineteenth centuries, the amount spent on the hangings and upholstery generally far exceeded the cost of the woodwork. The term furniture was, in the eighteenth century, used as much for hangings as well as movables.

Gradually, more luxurious forms of seating were designed: tall-backed chairs with some adjustments for reclining,, sofas with down-filled cushions and arms padded with horse-hair; chairs with upholstered and full length backs. Even the cane -seated chairs of the eighteenth century were generally made more comfortable with mattress-like squabs tied on with tapes. At this time French chairs differed in having domed stuffed seats and it was not until the 1780s when the neo-classical period was well advanced, that the French generally adopted squarer forms of stuffing to harmonise them with the linear neo-classical style.

TRIMMINGS

For trimming the edges of the upholstered chairs, fringes gave way to braids, often home-made. But the most usual form of chair edging during the second half of the eighteenth century was decorative brass nailing. Loosely fitting cotton covers were placed over the upholstery to protect precious materials from sunlight and dust when a room was not in use for a grand occasion, and such attention to conservation has ensured the survival of many important suites of upholstered furniture.

Below: An English George III mahogany sofa with tapestry upholstery c.1790-1800. In the last years of the eighteenth century, sofas became much squarer in form. Frequently the back and sides were completely upholstered, but this version has slim tapered legs which are extended to form the fronts of the arms. Note the padded seat and fringe decoration. Tapestry was still a popular upholstery material at this time, being woven in Britain as well as France.

TABLES

The eighteenth century was distinguished by its craftsmanship, and the quality of manufacture has never since been equaled. The influence of American designers and craftsman was also a force to be recognised during this time. Status in all countries could be embodied in the importance as well as the modishness of furniture, and so the most wealthy paid attention to developments in both comfort and convenience. Where they led, the general populace followed. Tables had started out in the earlier centuries as little more than trestles with long narrow boards resting on easily movable supports. In the seventeenth century they became shaped and adorned, while one aspect of changing styles in the eighteenth century saw an increase in the number and function of small tables represented.

DESIGN FOR FUNCTION

The range of types and styles of tables that developed in the eighteenth century is truly astonishing. France was an obvious leader in the field, notably developing small specialist tables such as table en chiffonière (a work table with a high gallery) and a table à ouvrage (for needlework). Tables de nuit were simple night-stands that stood beside the bed. Primarily designed to hold a chamber pot, they were used extensively throughout Europe in the second half of the century. Later models became increasingly sophisticated, using fake drawers and closing doors to disguise their real function.

'Guéridon' was a term used to refer to candle stands, but it was also applied to small round tables developed from same the basic shape. The wood-tripod guéridons were generally more popular in England than in France. The original design allowed for the narrow top to hold a candelabra, while the shaft sometimes allowed for adjustment of height. The style of table developed to the point where stretchers

Previous page: Table à ouvrage c. 1745 The top is leather covered, as are the drawers. The rococo decoration of elaborate inlay designs or organic motifs is in kingwood.

Below: Table de nuit c. 1750. This relatively discrete piece is from Louis XV's reign, an era better known for its ostentation,

evolved to be a second tier or shelf. Examples can be found in a variety of wood, and also in metal work. Guéridon could also be adapted purely for decoration. The name 'guéridon' is said to derive from a servant who gave his name to such candlesticks, and the term was later applied to small tables.

PRACTICAL DESIGNS

In many cases the decorative function of a table outweighed the practical. The gilded

seventeenth century console table was originally designed to fill an unseemly gap on the walls of the Galerie des Glaces (Hall of Mirrors) in Louis XIV's Versailles. Console tables are frequently found in pairs. Asymmetry was an essential element of Rococo design and these tables were an ideal medium to display it. Versailles is lined with these tables, alternating between windows and mirrors along the walls. Most are fairly square in shape with straight square-sectioned members. The

Bottom left: A Transitional guéridon c. 1760 The legs of this table gently curve from the 'knee' just under the frieze. It is made of tulipwood with herringbone cross-banding. Stretchers were not structurally necessary for a table of this design and a second tier has been introduced for decoration.

Bottom right: A French iron guéridon c. 1780. This example is close to the original function as a candle-stand. The adjustable shaft allowed the height of the light source to vary. The contemporary Englishman Matthew Boulton produced similar pieces, although they tended to be in gilt bronze of high quality following the trend for French ormolu.

Below: A Louis XVI giltwood console table c. 1780. This piece is very similar to many console tables used by Robert Adam in his interiors for the English aristocracy during the 1770s and 1780s. With a half-moon shape, and finely fluted legs the frieze is heightened by a guilloche and egg-and-tongue decoration, forms and motifs favored by the English. The French originals are evident in the stout legs and the stretcher is heavy.

Below right: A Louis XV gilt iron console table c. 1740. Not all craftsmen worked in wood. France had a lively tradition of iron-work which began in the sixteenth century and continues today. Iron stretchers were used in Spain as early as the seventeenth century, although metal furniture was adopted much later in Britain and America. This console table uses hammered steel to form a single cabriole leg. The pierced frieze imitates wood carving, but use of

metal allowed the craftsman greater experimentation. The decoration is made from thinner sheet metal. The scallop shell and pendant flowers have been cut as silhouettes and bent in to shape using gently applied heat.

Above: A Finnish pine dresser c. 1750 The uneven top and edges of this item are proof that the timber was cut with a primitive saw and adze probably used in shaping the pieces which were then pegged together. The lack of decoration indicates its purely functional purpose, but it can be clearly seen to be the basis for some forms of contemporary pine furniture today.

Left: A Louis XV coiffeuse c. 1750. The central panel pulls up to reveal a mirror, while three frieze drawers are compartmentalised. The slide above the middle drawer pulls out to hold the brushes.

Above: An English George III satinwood Hepplewhite dressing table c. 1780. Cunningly designed, this table is fitted with a dummy drawer. The hinged lid, decorated with neo-classical motifs of an urn surrounded by scrolls, lifts upwards to reveal a fitted interior. The stylishness of this piece could well be due to a habit women had at this time of receiving guests while dressing, thus requiring a dressing table that was both decorative and functional.

Above: A French Régence ebonised bureau plat c.1725 This is a leading form of writing table from the period. The cubic design epitomises the work of the French architect Joseph Berain (1638-1711). This design replaced the earlier, heavier style with inlaid brass and tortoise-shell. The ebonised effect comes from using paint and polish. The mounts are ormolu, but functional, and the top is leather.

Left: An American tea table, walnut, c. 1760. The tilting top of this Chippendale-style tea table is released by a 'birdcage' mechanism: the latch is surrounded by tiny turned columns like a cage. With sharply curving cabriole legs and ball-and-claw feet, the whole table has a refined elegant look, characteristic of pieces made in Philadelphia.

design of console tables would be integral to the decoration of the room..

DRESSING TABLES

Dressing tables take many shapes across Europe. In Finland, some mediaeval designs continued to be made up to the eighteenth and nineteenth centuries for everyday use. The continued popularity of traditional forms was due to a lack of tools and money, which meant that pieces had to be strictly functional. This also meant that they could be used to perform a variety of functions: table, seating, storage for valuables and food, etc. In France an extreme version evolved to be the coiffeuse. The name derives from the French verb 'coiffer', meaning to dress the hair. People sat before this specialist piece of furniture while

Left: An English George III mahogany architect's or drawing table c. 1780. This elegant work table is understated in design, indicated by the tapering legs and drawers. Educated Georgians were often concerned with the planning of their own properties, and this item is a concrete reminder of the interests of the time.

Below: A Louis XVI table à la bourgognone c. 1760. The tables à la bourgogne were a form of mechanical writing table popular in Paris in the 1760s. Cleverly designed, they were often packed with secret compartments which were revealed by pressing spring-operated hidden catches. When closed this table appears quite ordinary, with a deep marquetry frieze. When opened, however, a fitted interior appears, with four small drawers and recesses for stationery. Finely proportioned, this is a restrained, elegant design.

creating the elaborate hairstyles that were all the rage at the court of Louis XV. It would contain all the brushes and powders, needed, as well as a mirror too. English types of dressing tables may have had the appearance of a small commode with fitted drawers.

WRITING TABLES

Writing table took on several guises in the eighteenth century. The table à écrire, the bureau plat, and table à la bourgognone all

served a similar purpose, despite looking very different. The bureau plat was a precursor to the desk, whereas the table à écrire was a delicate table at which a lady might sit in her boudoir. The table à la bourgognone developed from a fascination with gadgetry in furniture in both England and France. Louis XVI had considerable influence on furniture design because of his interest in technical design and mechanical devices. This interest was shared by the Georgians in England and was also seen

in the design of their writing desks.

TABLES FOR ARCHITECTS

Continuing a fascination for mechanical furniture, architect's or artist's drafting tables were cleverly constructed and elegant in design, as well as being eminently practical. Adjustable tables were indicative of the contemporary vogue for sketching, water-colour and oil painting. Different mechanisms can be found which raised the working surface. The simplest design of two ratchets allowed the surface to be either flat or angled. When closed, some versions covered an aperture which could hold materials.

OCCASIONAL TABLES

The ornate courts of Louis XIV and XV saw the flowering of a myriad of small tables – the writing table, dressing table, occasional table, card tables, and after the introduction of tea from the Orient, the tea table. Contemporary social developments clearly influenced the need for separate items. Card tables usually came in sets of four. A classic format for card tables around 1785 was the D-shape. A rear leg hinged in the middle of the back swings out like a gatefold to support the top, which when unfolded usually revealed a baize lined interior. Earlier in the decade the demi-lune (or half-moon) shape was the preferred style.

Throughout the century, tables were commissioned to enhance the contemporary feel of a room, as well as for purely practical reasons. Many clients would have had considerable input to the overall design. The Pembroke table, according to Sheraton was named after the person who first commissioned one: 'who probably gave the first idea of such a table to the workmen'. Introduced during

Below: An English George III satinwood painted card table c. 1785 The second half of George III's reign is some times known as 'The Age of Satinwood' and is considered by many to be the finest period of English decorated furniture. This beautifully executed table probably one of a set of four would have been very expensive in its own time. It is covered in all types of

Georgian painted decoration, including a centre panel filled with musical trophies (instruments displayed artistically); the frame of floral garlands and ribbons, and the cross-banded edges of tulipwood and burr yew wood. The legs and sides are painted with similar motifs.

Left: An English George II Pembroke table c. 1780. This delicate table embodies Sheraton and Hepplewhite ideals of decoration. Made of sycamore, which itself has a shimmering grain, the table is cross-banded in tulipwood. The detail illustrates nearly the entire Georgian vocabulary of decoration: a large shell-shaped inlay is framed by an anthemion and urn-draped frieze scrolls; this in turn is surrounded by portrait medallions hung from ribbons and joined by swags of husks

Left: A French Régence side-table c. 1720. Clear signs of the Rococo influence are visible in this table: the tapering legs, and lightly curved stretchers. The deep frieze on the top gives the piece a vertical feel which makes it seem taller than it actually is, and the restrained decoration makes it feel lighter.

the 1750s, they have two flaps supported by hinge brackets and were originally rectangular, although later pieces are more often oval or have serpentine edges. Pembroke tables are practical items, as can be seen from Adam's designs: console and side tables were clearly for decoration but Pembroke tables were in constant domestic use.

FRENCH INFLUENCE

By 1730 in France a variety of tables was an essential and valued part of the furniture of the aristocratic household. During the Régence period there had been an increasing interest in the quality of manufacture as the range of decorative options declined. Stretchers were disappearing and veneering with plain wood grain and lacquering was on the rise. In no time a new curved style of which Régence is considered the first phase, fully emerged – Rococo. Typically, console tables stood on exaggeratedly curved legs, which would be decorated with foliage on the legs and a basket of flowers or a rococo scroll on the stretchers.

EUROPEAN DEVELOPMENTS

Italy and Germany followed the lead of France, especially when it came to the Rococo. The English trend for plain dark woods began with the use of native walnut and continued with the use of mahogany supplied by the colonies. After the 1720s this was available without duty. The new wood carved easily and yielded beautiful grain patterns, known as figuring. The Chippendale style developed with Rococo patterns applied to a plethora of English tables. Favoured motifs were leaf carvings, pierced lattice work and Chinese motifs. As an extension of the style, the fantasy element revived the Gothic, with a medieval cathedral evoked on a table whose legs might be carved as clusters of tectonic columns.

DESIGN FOR THE MASSES

The spate of pattern books started a new Anglomania. Thomas Chippendale's designs set a new fashion, and American cabinet-makers were also able to copy the designs of Sheraton and Hepplewhite well in to the nineteenth century.

Robert Adam's influence was popular in England and France in the 1760s and 1770s. In his designs tables often played a crucial part, frequently being fixed to a wall near windows to give symmetry to the formal room

Below: A marquetry table by David Roentgen c. 1785. This simple oval table with disguised drawer is typical of David Roentgen. He collaborated with a famous clock-maker Pierre Kintzing, and specialised in hidden drawers. In this case, one long drawer reveals four hidden ones when a secret catch is opened at the end of the table. Although the shape is clear, the inlay and colour on the top and sides detract from the simplicity of line. German craftsman attempted neo-classical pieces such as this perhaps because of the still-strong influence of the Rococo in Germany.

Below: A rosewood writing table by Thomas Chippendale c.1756. This beautiful and elegant table is rare because of its unusual kidney shape.The documents of its original sale still survive. It was made for Winifred Constable of Burton Constable, a large house with spectacular bay windows. The table may well have been designed to fit one of them. By Chippendale standards, it is discreet and uncluttered , with its decoration being the contrasting grains of the inlaid fan-shaped patterns.

Below right: An American federal candle-stand c.1785 This table was made specifically to hold candelabra and has a small drawer below to accommodate lighting equipment such as a tinder box and wax tapers. This table was probably made in Connecticut, and is of red cherry wood with a beautiful even grain. The beginning of neo-classical influence can be seen in the fan shaped inlay on the top and urn-like column and the graceful angular tripod with small feet which are known as pointed snake feet.

layouts. Straight lines characterised the table style of the 1780s, which were enhanced with fluted legs in the style of Roman temples. The tops and aprons tended to be flatter and more restrained, made of plain mahogany with simple geometric inlay.

In America settlers used tables brought from their homeland, but more often used the native woods to make tables in the style of the Old World. Simple Puritan values of plain unfettered practical designs were a heavy influence, but after Independence distinctive colonial table production began to emerge. By 1800 North America boasted thriving centres of high quality production of European-style tables, incorporating local variations. Concentrated in New England, Philadelphia and New York,

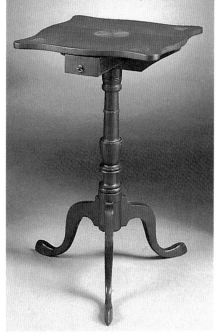

their work is still sought after today.

MATERIALS AND DECORATION

Diversity in table function, size and construction provided great scope for interpretation. Flat surfaces and straight lines are open to endless decoration and ornament, and craftsmen and designers drew from sources such as religion, archaeology and nature for their inspiration. The designs of the eighteenth century were clearly indicative of the breadth of influence

Function and decoration are obvious ways to classify tables, but the materials used are also extremely important. In Europe native woods such as oak and walnut were used as they were dense and durable. The tradition of

Below left: English yew table, c. *1710. Yew was often used as an alternative to walnut. This is a typical Queen Anne-period table. The tightly patterned grain, and yellow-gold colour provide a subtle accompaniment to the simple shape of this table. The top is inlaid with the design of a house. It is surrounded by a cushioned edge and an undecorated frieze. Supported by straight legs ending in pad feet, the lack of stretchers gives the table a lighter feel. The only ornament is the slight scroll where the leg and apron meet.*

Below: An Italian gilt side table c. 1700. The strong Italian carving tradition meant most artists and craftsman could turn their hands to carving decoration. The carving on this table is natural in form, with central scallop shells demonstrating the roots of the rococo movement. The legs are scrolling, dolphin-like forms, and the support seems rather large for such a small marble top. It is likely that this is not original to the piece.

Below: An Italian Louis XV Lacca contrafatta side table c. 1760. The decoration of this table is uniquely Italian as is the sculptural quality: the Louis XV cabriole legs start with an angelic head at the top and the feet are carved into leafy hooves. It is a variant on the chiffonière.

Above: A Chinese hardwood altar table, 1760. This is a high-quality piece and shows an unusual amount of decoration and extensive carving. The top is pierced with naturalistic designs of the branches of the Prunus tree.

carving developed in the Renaissance was readily adapted to new harder woods arriving from the colonies. While ebony, zebra and rosewoods were used for veneers to stunning effect, it was the designs of Chippendale that made the best possible use of mahogany, revealing the fine grain and deep colour.

In France two gifted craftsmen Charles Cressen (1685-1768) and Bernard van Risenburgh (1730-1770) lead the way to a new golden age of furniture making. New look tables had eccentric curving, light hearted constructions in pale-coloured woods (often with parts cut out) and, especially in France, finely chiselled gilt-bronze or ormolu, mounts.

THE ITALIAN JOB

Italian craftsmen had a penchant for unrestrained decoration of furniture. Painting of landscapes, flowers and figures was a favourite form. They adopted japanning as an alternative to oriental lacquer, but went on to develop their own interpretation. The technique known as 'lacca povera' (or 'lacca contrafatta') involved pasting cut-out and painted pictures – chinoiserie or rustic scenes were most often used – on the painted surface and then lavishly coating the whole with varnish.

A group of outstanding craftsmen gathered in Turin in the 1730s. Brought together by Filippo Juvarra to work on the Palazzo Reale, they include the sculptor Francesco Ladatte and the cabinet-maker Pietro Piffetti. They produced well made, and highly ornamental pieces. Much Italian furniture in the eighteenth century was influenced by French artists, particularly in the areas of Piedmont and Liguria. On the whole, designs were exaggerated and larger than life – curves were greater, decoration more colourful.

Piffetti's confection of inlaid ivory, mother

of pearl and exotic woods with finely chiseled bronze mounts was one of the earliest example lightening the baroque style and transforming it into the Rococo. It led to the enthusiastic adoption of bombé fronts and serpentine shapes. Any defects in the craftsmanship could be easily disguised with gay painting,, lacca, or lavish gilding.

The links with the Orient also had a lasting effect, not only with the import of materials, but also through the unusual and delicate artworks. Tables had been used in China since the days of the T'Ang Dynasty (AD 618-906), although they served a different purpose to those in Europe. They were often used in pairs and set along walls to hold incense burners or Chinese lutes. In a formal setting they were placed on the east or west walls, but in a less formal setting they may have been placed asymmetrically.

Generally, Chinese tables changed very little, but increasing western influence was seen in the development of decoration. Chinese furniture tended to follow simple elegant lines and fit together without dowels or nails. Increased trade with colonial outposts brought enormous wealth to many aristocrats and merchants, some of which was inevitably spent on commissioning furniture to decorate their increasingly lavish homes.

Left: Florentine scagliola table top, 1756. This table top is one of a signed pair, and is inscribed DP Belloni A Florentine F 1756 ('Don Pietro Belloni made this at Florence in 1756'). Using light colours and showing shells, flowers and small animals, it is an example of Rococo at its best. In 1790 scagliola was much in demand as a cheap way of imitating rare marble. It was used by both Robert Adam and George Smith.

DESKS AND CABINETS

In 1650 most writing in England and America would have been done at a table, or at a simple table top desk. By 1750 it was possible to choose from a range of established types of desk. Before this time desks were only commonplace in churches, monasteries and palaces, because reading and writing played little part in people's lives. Writing furniture played no real part in the mainstream until the eighteenth century when a great variety was to be found in the homes of well-to-do people. Another important development in eighteenth century furniture was the evolution of the chest on a stand to the large bureau cabinet. Portable writing boxes evolved into small cabinets with flaps and drawers, to desk and bookcase combinations known as bureau-cabinets.

Previous page: An English Queen Anne oak bureau c. 1710. This example of a simple compact desk is equipped with a stepped interior and a well beneath the fall-front. Plain, honest oak pieces such as this continued to be made by country craftsmen throughout the eighteenth century.

Below: An English portable table desk c. 1730. The carcass is made of pine, red japanned and decorated with chinoiserie in gold and silver. Under the flap are five drawers, three pigeon holes and a single base drawer cut from sold beech.

DESK STYLES

In 1755 Dr. Samuel Johnson published his *Dictionary of the English Language.* In it he defined several forms of writing furniture, but the most basic is the desk which he described as 'an inclining table for the use of writers or readers and made commonly with a box or repository underneath it'. This seems to have been virtually the only form of writing furniture found in homes before the middle of the seventeenth century. Boxes of this kind remained standard equipment for the traveler throughout the eighteenth and nineteenth centuries.

WRITING BOXES

Made in all qualities ranging from basic boxes to compendiums of elaborate presentation, writing boxes often featured fold-out writing slopes, adjustable reading stands, inkwells, pounce pots, even candleholders. This style was to become one of the building blocks for more complicated writing furniture. By the time Johnson published his dictionary, (itself a pioneering work for the increasingly literate middle classes) the proliferation of desks in

the homes of the upper classes proved that the skills of reading and writing were already important.

WRITING TABLES

While tables solely intended for writing were found in Italian palaces in the sixteenth century, the new forms did not have much of an impact in Britain till several centuries later.

Gate-leg tables with a fold out flap provided a starting point. A simple slope-fronted desk on a stand with a hinge at the bottom was the prototype of the slope-fronted bureau standard before 1700.

Below: A French Louis XV bureau plat c. 1730 Made by a leading ébéniste of the period, Charles Cressent, this bureau retains stately quality. It measures 6ft 9in in length. The Rococo decoration has the characteristic C-scroll for drawer handles, with sprigs of wayward leaves and a sweep of the central escutcheon. It has a leather-lined top, three frieze drawers and is mounted with finely modelled caryatids at the angles and bearded masks flanking the central drawer.

Inset: An English walnut-veneered table bureau c. 1705. The diamond and leaf inlaid fall-front opens to a fitted interior and forms a writing surface supported on a pair of tiny lopers with ring handles. This desk is a slightly more sophisticated reminder of the simple slope-topped boxes of the previous century.

EUROPEAN TRENDS

Much eighteenth century furniture was very feminine; tables for sewing, reading and writing reflected the middle and upper class woman's occupation in the home. When a large desk was required (generally for use by the male householder) a simple bureau plat was always popular in France and could be used in conjunction with a separate filing cabinet or catonnier.

The French equivalent of the slope-fronted desk was the free-standing bureau en pente, which was popular in 1750, but was soon displaced by the secrétaire à cylindre and the secrétaire à abattant. This upright form of the fall-front desk came back into favour, and lent itself to the classical rectangular shapes characterised by Louis XVI and the French Empire style of the early nineteenth century.

France also led the way in providing women with a great variety of well thought-out smaller writing tables for everyday use. Small slope-fronted bureaux for ladies appeared on both sides of the Channel early in the eighteenth century, but in Paris ébénistes showed the greatest ingenuity and virtuosity in creating little tables à écrire. These were often work tables or delicate dressing tables which contained spaces for pen, ink, paper and a writing surface. No other writing furniture illustrates more the importance of written communication in the pre-telephone era. The French also created the most distinctive and practical of all desks for women, the bonheur du jour, which was taken up in Britain with enthusiasm, and enjoyed a great vogue among French ladies in the 1760s.

In the very best writing furniture produced by the Paris ébénistes, there is an attention to detail seldom found elsewhere. Creations such as the Bureau de Roi, created for Louis XV

Below: An English tulipwood bonheur du jour c. 1775. The neo-classical marquetry is in the Adam style. The upper section contains two small cupboards, with the oval paterae on the doors and a single shelf with a three-quarter brass gallery. The serpentine main section is decorated around the frieze with stylized flowers and festoons and contains a single drawer.

Below: The Bureau de Roi Louis XV. This bureau was made for the study of Louis XV and took nine years to complete. It was started by Jean François Oeben in 1760, and finished by his successor Jean Henri Riesener. The exterior is dominated by magnificent gilt-bronze mounts and decorated with marquetry panels. Evidence suggests that the blue and white biscuit de Sèvres plaque of the Three Graces replaced royal ciphers which were defaced during the Revolution. In common with many other Paris-based German craftsmen, Oeben loved mechanical intricacies. In this desk the tambour slides open at the touch of a button to reveal small drawers flanking pigeon holes and a writing surface. The center panel is raised by a button to form a reading stand, and beneath it is a well containing three drawers. A secret drawer exists on the left-hand side of the interior.

by Oeben and finished by his successor Reisener, combined elegance, convenience and ingenuity to a standard that was unmatched even by the tour de force exhibition pieces seen in Europe a century later.

The Bureau de Roi was in itself a technical innovation and the many mechanical surprises it embodies are a reminder that eighteenth century France was fascinated by science and technology, but such mechanical intricacy was expensive. The limited means of the middle classes in France and elsewhere were stretched to more modest interpretations of court style.

LIBRARY AND OFFICE FURNITURE

In the library, a specialised room of growing importance in the eighteenth century, large pedestal desks that could be placed in the centre of the book-lined room were found most convenient. Library furniture tended towards the monumental. The Gothic revival was particularly well suited to library furniture: tall shelving, and imposing desks lent themselves to an architectural treatment.

Partners' desks were intended to be free standing, and could be used in a library or office. Their name derived because they had

Below: An English mahogany library writing table c. *1758 This desk is characteristic of the Gothic revival that took place in the mid-eighteenth century. The desk has a leather inset top supported on four pedestals decorated with medallions of applied Gothic tracery and with engaged cluster columns at the corners. There are three shallow drawers in the frieze, and three drawers are hidden behind a door of solid mahogany in each pedestal.*

drawers on both sides and partners could sit opposite each other. Clerks' desks barely changed in two centuries and desks of similar designs were to be found in schools until the middle of the twentieth century.

BUREAU CABINETS

In Britain the large bureau cabinet with drawers beneath and paper storage above was a standard piece by mid-century. There were many variations in design and size. Some examples were double domed, while others had a straight cornice. The arrangement of storage space varied, and a central recessed cupboard sometimes replaced the more customary drawer arrangement

The most striking lacquer-decorated bureau book-cases of the early eighteenth century were architectural in style and designed to stand against a wall. Sometimes a pair of mirrored doors concealed shelves or small compartments, other styles had plain veneered or japanned doors. Such pieces were designed to grace the grand salons of large houses. The design was ideally suited to the everyday business of a household, and it was adaptable. Later in the century the upper part tended to be glazed, but the form of the typical English bureau meant it could also be dispensed with altogether without spoiling the appearance or usefulness of the desk.

Smaller versions with single doors in the upper part were popular for use in a ladies' bedrooms or dressing rooms. Although the little kneehole dressing-table-cum-desk was also common.

AMERICAN STYLE

In America elegant writing furniture in the form of the slope-front desks and book cases were part of the move towards a comfortable

Below: An English Queen Anne lacquered bureau cabinet. This desk is typical early eighteenth century. The commanding double domed cabinet has anchored mirror panels on the doors used to magnify the light of candles placed on slides above the fall front. Decoration is chinoiserie style, of birds, figures in landscapes and flowering plants. Exotic japanned furniture remained popular in the early part of the century.

Below: An English George III clerk's desk in mahogany. The leather inlaid writing slope forms the hinged lid to a compartment containing two small drawers. There is also a full width drawer and shaped gallery in the base.

life. The bureau-cabinet was a favourite form. It became one of the most representative pieces of East Coast cabinet furniture, developing subtle but distinct regional characteristics.

This popular form was also adopted in much of Europe, .A distinctive Dutch form with profuse marquetry decoration and a heavy bombé base with canted projecting corners remained popular throughout the 1700s, while German and Italian craftsmen developed fantastic Rococo forms.

Right: An English mahogany veneered bureau cabinet c. 1755 This eccentric piece is also large. The poor workmanship suggests a provincial cabinet-maker, but the design is unique. The upper part is in the form of a pyramid with six graduated shelves enclosed by a pair of doors adorned on either side with mezzo-tints of great English poets. Beneath this is the fall-flap with a fitted interior. The base has eight shallow drawers above and below cupboards decorated with mezzo-tints of ancient scholars.

COMMODES

The commode (chest of drawers) was the principle piece of case furniture of the period. It had a curved front, sides and legs, and either two or three rows of drawers. As the Transitional and neo-classical styles developed, the body of a commode was adorned with formal flower marquetry and a severe scroll frieze. Gilt-bronze corner mounts were sometimes modeled on the triglyph, and the mounts on the apron were modelled on a smoking cassolette (incense vessel).

With the reign of Louis XVI case furniture acquired an angular look. Commodes were often square, although some examples are half-moon shapes or have a break-front façade in which the central part of the façade is shaped as a projecting panel.

Provincial versions are only rarely found with the full bombé shape of the sophisticated Louis XV pieces, but many are shaped from side to side in serpentine or arc-en-arbalète (crossbow) form. Some are richly carved, but many are relatively plain, with wooden, rather than marble tops.

DISPLAY CABINETS

The Dutch passion for porcelain led to the

Right: An American Chippendale mahogany slope-front desk c. 1765-80. This desk design is attributed to John Townsend of Newport, Rhode Island. It has a shell-carved blockfront interior of small drawers pigeonholes, and a cupboard. The substantial curved bracket feet are typical of the Townsend style, midway between the simple bracket feet of Queen Anne period and the showy ball and claw which characterised Chippendale style.

Left: French commode, kingwood and gilt, c. 1753. This commode is a fine example of the bold gilt and bronze mounts favoured by its maker Charles Cressent who was France's most talented cabinet-maker of the Régence period.

Below left: Dutch display cabinet, walnut, mid-eighteenth century. This piece features carved cresting in the Rococo style and decoratively scrolled glazing bars.

Below: American mahogany highboy, c. 1760. The shell carving identifies this piece as a fine example of New England furniture-making.

invention of the glass-fronted display cabinet. Corner cupboards, some with lacquered panels in the doors were also used for displaying china. Both types were adopted in England.

Corner cupboards were really smaller relatives of bookcases. In America they appeared in the early eighteenth century in either simple pine or walnut with a carved shell top. Their shape often echoed architectural styles, and many surviving American pieces are painted.

DECORATION
Pictorial marquetry continued to be used, and popular motifs were ruins of landscapes, exotic objects, such as Chinese tableware, and complex geometric patterns. Gradually, however, plain veneer especially in mahogany began to supplant marquetry. Well-figured woods, outlined with finely chiseled gilt, bronze, were used as was oriental lacquer. Panels of pietra dura or boulle marquetry often

Below: Italian commode, walnut, mid-eighteenth century. The exuberant inlays and decoration of ivory, mother of pearl, and gilt metal on this north Italian bombé commode belong to a style already popular in the seventeenth century. Together with the elegant handles and escutcheons, the inlaid flowers and other motifs illustrate the enthusiasm for decorative effect.

scavenged from other furniture were fixed to commodes and cabinets and given surrounds of ebony veneer. Plaques of Sèvres porcelain were also applied to case furniture.

In Spain and Portugal marquetry was generally detailed and delicate, although painting and gilding were used, and metal mounts were seldom seen. The Portuguese gave a distinctive interpretation of rococo to commodes and beds, with an emphasis on embellishments in carved wood. Portuguese commodes were taller than those in other European countries, nearly always with a depth of four drawers. German commodes were veneered with tortoiseshell or exotic timbers or decorated with marquetry of wood, mother of pearl, ivory and sometimes silver. They were profusely ornamental, with gilt-bronze mounts.

In Russia the most fashionable styles were enthusiastically adopted for palaces and

Below: Portuguese commode, late eighteenth century. This piece, known as the 'Donna Maria commode', is typified by its linear design, finely crafted marquetry, a deep apron and a marble top.

country houses. Peter the Great's efforts to introduce European cultural influences to Russia saw an influx of foreign craftsmen. Many respected cabinet makers working in Russia were German migrants. Some were imbued with the ideals of David Roentgen's workshop, and they had a major influence on the development of neo-classicism in Russia.

A blend of mid-European styles and peculiarly Russian characteristics developed during the eighteenth century and lasted for well over a hundred years.

MARCHANDS-MERCIERS

In eighteenth century France a group of dealers known as 'marchands-merciers' supplied furniture and decorative objects to a rich clientele desperate to keep up with the latest trends. They exerted considerable influence not only on the making of furniture, but also on its design. They eventually came to control the work of all specialists involved in the creation of pieces of furniture.

Dominique Daguerre, the greatest mercier of the late eighteenth century, commissioned

Below: American blanket chest, 1789. This painted, two door blanket chest was made by Johannes Rank All the painted motifs had symbolic meanings relating to love, marriage, religion, and fertility.

Left: American highboy, mahogany, 1760. The shell carving on this beautiful highboy identifies it as a typical example of New England furniture making.

Below: French cherrywood commode c. 1740 This provincial chest of drawers has a carved frieze and arc-en-arbalète (cross-bow) front

drawings, ordered porcelain plaques of specific shape and decoration from the Sèvres factory, bought lacquer cabinets that were then dismantled for their panels, and arranged for gilt-bronze mounts to be made by leading metal workers. This left only the making of the carcass and the final assembly to the ébeniste, (cabinet-maker) who was thus reduced from designer to executor.

THE PENNSYLVANIAN TRADITION

During the eighteenth century the groups who had settled in America turned their energies to the creation of idiomatically made and decorated furniture. Among the customs brought from Europe was the tradition of the dower chest, given by the parents and friends to the daughter of the family. Made to houses homespun linens, quilts, hangings and towels for a future marriage, the chests were painted to order. Background shades of soft blue, green, black or brown were used and decorated motifs from medieval myths and Christian legend. Symbols included unicorns (virginity), hearts (love), mermaids (sex), the tree of life (mortality), flowers (fertility), doves (peace), and the pelican and fish (Christ). Several chests carry the owner's name or the initials and the date it was made. Most artists were unknown although the records of two survive: Christian Selzer (1749-1831) and Heinrich Otto.

Another particular piece of furniture was the Schrank, a heavy wardrobe of thick planks which was ornately painted or inlaid with the usual

Below: A mahogany American bureau, c. 1760-70. The vigorous lines of Queen Anne style are clear in this elegant block-front bureau. The blocking on the front suggests that it was made in Rhode Island. It is a technique that emphasizes the quality of the wood as the undulating surface reflects every change in the light.

mythological symbols, or more temporal motifs such as crowns and swastikas. Schranks and cupboards were usually supported on ball or bracket feet.

Further removed from the centre of European fashion, style on the American continent would have seemed more conservative. However, they developed distinctive characteristics like the bonnet tops on desks, bookcase and highboys

The highboy was a chest of drawers with the upper section standing on the lower section with legs. In its first incarnation during the William and Mary period, the highboy was usually made of walnut and had six, rarely four, spindle or ball-and-cone turned legs connected by stretchers and terminating in ball feet. With the appearance of Queen Anne style, the six spindle legs developed into four cabriole legs, and turned pendant knops decorated the apron. The ogee suited the proportions of the piece and in the 1730s the curve of the apron became more pronounced; eventually the flat top acquired a pediment. Walnut gave way to mahogany in popularity, except in Philadelphia.

Below: American corner cupboard, blue-painted wood, early eighteenth century. Cupboards such as this with a glazed upper door and receded columns in the early Federalist mode are extremely collectable.

Below: Dutch bureau-cabinet. Dating from the middle of the eighteenth century, this piece exhibits the strong proportions and exuberant marquetry that has come to be associated with Dutch cabinet-making.